Thoughts and Prayers

Thoughts and Prayers

A Collection of Poetic Inspiration

Stephen Remillard II

Cover Design: Dan Verkys
Works Collected by: Stephen Remillard
Edited: Shelley Mascia

ISBN: 978-0-578-82358-4
EISBN: 978-0-578-82359-1

Dedication:

These works were collected with a simple motivation. To provide a bit of encouragement to the reader and to give an offering to the Children's Cancer Foundation. The authors represented here have donated their time, emotion, and written word to assist in this endeavor. Presented herein are some of the kindest hearts I have ever had the honor of getting to know. It is my sincere hope that this collection can lend some strength in one of life's most unfair struggles.

Best wishes to all.

Stephen Karl Remillard II

Mentions:

Kris AlKantara	*Instagram Krisassy.101*
Jana Begovic	*Facebook.com/J.Damselfly/*
Charlene Ann Benoit	*Facebook.com/charleneannbenoit*
Danny Boy	*Facebook.com/DannyBoyPoetry*
Kathy Brinley	
Caroline Carter	*Instagram carolinecarterpoetry*
Eva Coffey	*Facebook.com/CoffeyLoveNook*
Pooja Francis	
Darlene Gregg	*Facebook Ramblings of a Winter Rose*
Mira Hadlow	*Facebook.com/mirahadloww*
Debbie Hainey	*Facebook Winldflower Afternoons*
Laura Hughes	*Facebook Words Spilled From My Heart*
Will Hoeye	*Facebook.com/LordThyrm77*
Catherine McGrew Jaime	
Emily James	*Facebook.com/akaemilyjames*
CAJ	*Facebook Kindred Souls*
Antony King	*F acebook.com/ADarkerSideOfPoetry*
Kimberly Krausman	*Instagram eye_of_iris*
Brandy Lane	*Facebook.com/wherebeautifullives*
Theresa Louw	*Facebook Impassioned Heart*
Jeff Oliver	*Facebook Words from the Soul*
Donnie Pike	*Facebook A Poet's Journey*
Lisa Pilgrim	*Facebook Priceless Words by Lisa Pilgrim*
Stephen Remillard	*Facebook.com/sharedthoughts69*
Gypsy's Reverie	*Facebook Gypsy's Reverie*
Vaughn Roste	*Twitter @Vaughn09187022*
Michelle Schaper	*Facebook.com/Chellessoulpoems/*
Dennis Shepherd	*Facebook Deep Thought & Poetry*
Pam Surface	
Melissa A. Tafoya	*Facebook TheGypsyFliesWithSweetMelissa*
Ann Christine Tabaka	*https://annchristinetabaka*

Diana L Thomas *Facebook.com/dianajumpedup*
Melody Wang
Christine S Weir
Hanlie Wheeler
Linda J Zimmerman

TO MY BROTHER

Should you go out tonight, please don't forget
Unless it rained or when the clouds went green
Bring a jar, a cookie jar and the net
Should you go out tonight, please don't forget
Catch me some stars and some moonlight, my pet
It might not rain, the sky is tangerine
Should you go out tonight, please don't forget
Unless it rained or when the clouds went green

Kris AlKantara

In My Dream...

I wondered in solitude through lavender fields,
Drunk on mystery, magic, moonlight, and dreams,
Shedding the thorns grown from grief's bitter seeds,
Stringing around my heart faith's glittering beads,
Remembering again to dance to the rhythm of the rain,
While listening to the sweet cadences of my soul's pain,
Memories of how once my giddy heart had leapt and trilled,
Fused with the colours of the sky and the caress of the wind,
Breathings of the Earth seeped anew into my bones,
Until carefree I danced in a moonlit circle of stones,
The ancient forests in my dream whispered that all would be well,
I trusted their promise feeling hope and gratitude within me swell,
In my dream I relearned the secret language of my own soul,
And felt the miracle of being renewed, healed and whole.

Jana Vasilj-Begovic

Hope

Day after day another storm cloud,
Unable to feel the warmth of the sun,
Wiping away tears as though we're ashamed,
We need to stay strong for our little ones.

We hold back the rivers and give them smiles,
Mustering strength,
Whatever it takes,
As if faith will be lost to a moment of weakness,
The second they see our hearts break.

We brush fallen eyelashes off their cheeks,
Make wishes that the hard times will pass,
Waiting for good news to finally arrive,
Instead of the darkness that seems to amass.

Through the many trials and tribulations,
Hope is the one thing we can't let go.
It doesn't matter how many tears we cry...
If we lose it,
They just know.

Charlene Benoit

We are one

We are but a drop of water,
Yet together we are the whole ocean.

We are the tides and waves
shaping and carving the land.

We are each a grain of celestial sand
Which unite to compose beaches

We are the white noises
That conduct the songs of the cosmos

We are the primal forces
Which, in their forges
Form and cast the valleys
And great mountains

We are the reverberation
Of everything before us,
And the resonation
Of everything to come.

We are the cosmic dust
Which binds all things.
Living or dead,
Physical or ethereal,
Known or unknown.

We are separated,
Yet we are connected,
By the immutable power

Of the universe.
By love.

Danny Boy

Starlight Dreams

With starlight dreams
And moonlight glow
I'll always be with you
No matter where you go.

Fighting for you fiercely
Just like my love
It's strong
And on the days that seem dimly lit
I'll help you carry on.

Our bond is forged like rivers that move swiftly to the sea
And no matter how hard your day may be
You can always count on me.

I'll love you and I'll hold you close
And walk right by your side
I'll be the strength that carries you
No matter the mountains size.

Through ups and downs and
Everything
That could possibly come along
I'll be right here beside you
Through each day's new dawn.

My love for you is endless
Like the light of each full moon
And every star we wish upon
Will be for dreams come true.

So, rest your head upon my chest
Hear my heart beat true
Know that every dream I have
Is filled with love for you.

Every heartbeat that you hear
Echoing back into your own
Is what will help us move into
Another day's new dawn.

So sleep upon my chest tonight
My precious little babe
I'll hold you gently while you rest
And be here when you wake.

Kathy Brinley

"The two most important days in your life are the day you are born and the day you find out why."

Mountains

All these mountains that we climb
I'll paint them blue to match your eyes
And all those bad days left behind
I'll sing as symphonies to the blind
But know this too.
When you are weary
And can't see the mountains masterpiece
When deaf ears steal the music
Like a vagabond thief
I promise you, it is then
I'll take your hand and won't let go
Through the darkness of this life
I'll be sure we make it home

Caroline Carter

Awestruck

I am in awe of you
You have suffered extreme pain
You have gone through endless turmoil
You have known death face to face
Your body ravaged by the sickness within
But still, with battered soul you fight
You fight for all those dreams and hopes

One day you'll give wide smiles
Back on the lips of your dearest ones
Even with hearts so wounded
They have never given up
They have always believed
Giving their very all
Day and night so you can live
With your strength and determination
With your trust and faith in God
You hold on to their love
And you continue to fight
Oh, how I am in awe of you
Awestruck in humbled gratitude

Eva Coffey

Grow Hope

Sometimes the road gets too rough
You have no choice, but to get through that rough patch
In times like these

I hope you don't give up.

No matter how positive you are
Some things will go wrong and out of your hands
In times like these

I hope you don't give up.

Sometimes the person who was your last hope, walks away
Never mind
Because sometimes when people grow, they grow apart
In times like these

I hope you don't give up.

The trees you look around were just a tiny seed one day
And you say you don't believe in miracles?
You're just growing
So please

I hope you don't give up.

Sometimes when you take 1 step forward
Life pulls you 5 steps backwards
Don't worry
Even though life hasn't been fair, but when it pulls you back
It is only because you're going to be launched in some better place

So please don't ever give up.

Pooja Francis

HOPE

She is...
galaxies..
Worlds within worlds
With billions of stars
That dance brightly
Around the moonlight

She is...
the happiest smile
Tucked away in a bottle
That she wears
Around her neck

She is...
A melody made of
Steady notes
Smooth and perpetual
A song you want to hear
Over again

She is...
existence
Hands locked
With a side smile
Sweet, nurturing
She belongs here

She is...
eternity
Her grace
Is timeless..

Her existence
Breathes hope
That courses through
Her veins..

She is...
Pure magic
The cool breeze
That tickles your hair
Against your neck
In the deep woods
She is the fireflies
In the dark
Of night

She is...
Every woman
Every flower
Every season
The honey
In your tea..

.....and she lives
Inside you
and me

Darlene Gregg

My Way

And when I felt a little lost,
when the path
seemed to churn
and swirl at my feet,
when my heart was heavy
with questions
I didn't know how to ask.
When my soul was weary,
and uncertainty
dug barbs into my aching feet,
it was then that I knew
it was time.

It was time
to forsake the path,
to run unabashedly and wild
through forests and jungles.

It was time
to shake off the shackles
of all I ought to be.

It was time
to be as lost as I was able,
and it was only then
that I ever truly found
my way.

Mira Hadlow

Sweet Dreams

Grab on to the silver stars in the sky,
Lasso the royal moon up high...
Feel the strength of the Autumn breeze...
Take a ride on the colored, swirling leaves...
Feel the peace of the raindrops as they fall where they will...
Lay your pretty head on your pillow,
Listen to the sound of the Whippoorwill...

Debbie Hainey

I Believe...

I believe the sun will arise,
bringing a new light to your eyes.
I believe that with the new dawn,
hope springs forth, so you can move on.

I believe after the sun sets,
the day will end without regrets.
I believe as day turns to night,
everything will be all right.

I believe the stars and the moon,
have the power to make you swoon.
I believe their beauty shines bright,
because in darkness, we see light.

I believe wishes can come true,
as long as you want them to.
I believe in miracles too,
as every day begins anew.

Laura Hughes

Exist

Time ends
I will not
My soul continues.
Tear me down
Burn me
Scar me
I am forever
I AM!

Hope

Screaming
Begging
Crying
Fear is all they are
But I am better
I am stronger
I AM!

Alive

Pain is fleeting
Hurt fades
Even this ends.
And time starts again
Because
I AM!

Will Hoeye

Hope for Tomorrow

Amy held her little girl in her arms and rocked. Slowly at first but more quickly, then quicker, as the minutes ticked by. Some nights were worse than others and this had turned out to be a rough one. The four-year-old had tossed and turned between the bouts of nauseaousness brought on by the recent round of chemo.

She had finally gone to her and carried her to the well-used rocking chair in the family room. There she went through her repertoire of lullabies, glad that, at four, her daughter didn't think she was too old to be sung to. The tired, achy body relaxed the second time through "Swing Low, Sweet Chariots." But it wasn't until "Michael, Row the Boat Ashore" that the little eyes finally stopped fluttering open.

Amy looked down at her sleeping daughter, a look of contentment on the little face. The doctors had told them she was responding well to the chemo. There really was hope for a brighter tomorrow for this sweet little girl.

She smiled slightly and sang her daughter's favorite song again, this time for herself. "Jesus loves the little children, all the children of the world."

Yes, tomorrow would be a better day.

Catherine McGrew Jaime

Wildfire

Determination burns in me like a wildfire out of control
I have too much to do before this flame of mine burns out

There are mountains I need to climb
I want to climb high enough to reach the stars

I want to chase waterfalls and feel their power pulse through my veins
I need to run in fields of wildflowers barefoot and feel the dirt between my toes

I want to bid the moon good night then kiss the dawn good morning
There's puddles left to jump in and I want to slow dance in the rain

I want to feel the magic that only Christmas brings and catch snowflakes on my tongue

I have a mind and spirit full of determination and a heart and soul overflowing with hope

There's life left in me and I intend to live it
I won't stop until I'm done

Emily James

Mornings Story

I watched in awe this morning

To the rise of an early sun,

In all its grand, and gory,

As a new day had begun.

The fog had gently lifted,

And the earth became alive...

With a palette full of wonder

In hues of great delight.

For the beauty of this moment

In this scene that has unfold...

With loving strokes of the master's touch...

Mornings story has been told.

Antony King

In Dreams

Come Little One and sit with me,
Tell me your hopes and dreams.
Share with me where the rainbow ends,
And Unicorns prance on golden streets.

Take me to the forest's edge-
With trees so tall and green.
Lead me through the wooded trails
'Till we find the magical stream.

We will dance in the shallows,
And wash away what couldn't be healed.
We will celebrate your victory
Against this worldly spell.

Some may not believe us,
Until we show them that it's true.
Yet, we know it is not a secret...
What the power of love can do.

Kimberly Krausman

You Know My Heart

I've had much pain.
I've been through trials.
Through you I've found the strength,
to lift my head and smile.

I've had my doubts,
and my moments of weakness.
Instead, I'd like to remember,
all the moments I have been blessed.

You are there for me
when I am on my knees,
begging you for mercy.

You hold my hand.
You understand.
You know my very heart.

You will always be my everything,
my light in times of darkness.
I will push you away, and go astray,
but you'll call me back again.
You know my heart.

When I was told
to cherish the moments,
that I had left with my loved ones...
I just sat there for awhile.
It's as if I was given a life sentence,

I just couldn't believe that my days

were marked for an end.
I reached out for my husband,
my mother, my best friends...

and they were there for me,
through everything,
as I was begging you for mercy.

They held my hand
but didn't understand,
the pain I had inside.

They reminded me
that you're my everything,
my light in times of darkness.

They prayed for me
while I was on my knees,
holding back the tears.
They knew my heart

Guess you shined through me,
even when I didn't think you were there,
even when I lost my strength,
my energy, my hair.

Somehow you stayed with me,
held me in your hands,
and showed me what true beauty was
you made me understand.

That you are there for me
when I am on my knees,

begging you for mercy.

You hold my hand.
You understand.
You know my very heart.

You will always be my everything,
my light in times of darkness.
I will push you away, and go astray,
but you'll call me back again.

You know my heart.
You know my heart.

Brandy Lane

Her Soul

Through the looking glass
the windows of her soul
One could only see
lost hope and dreams
buried
in galaxies beneath
the silence of deafening screams
a soul so weak and weary
left numb by the monsters
trying to make believe
she is just another ordinary woman

fight beautiful one
fight
they are the weak ones
the monsters
hiding behind angel faces
they are the slaves of anger
they are unrequited love
they are abuse
they are hate
they are sickness
they are fake
trying to take
your rightful place
believe beautiful one
believe
you are strong
you are beautiful
you are kind
you belong

come sit with me
let's clean your looking glass
fill your soul with hope once more
I see you
the brightest reflection
of who you are
let it all go
find your courage
to breathe new hope
to live
to love
to laugh
to be
to take and own
your rightful place
In a bright new future
and the beauty of the unknown

- theresa louw -

Be Grateful

Look into their eyes
you can see
there is not an ounce of greed
look into their smiles
can you believe
they don't care about material things
you can't tell me
your life is so hard
when their bleeding
smiling through their scars
be grateful
for everything you are

Look into their dreams
you could find
the true meaning of your life
look into yourself
can you see
life's not that bad of a tragedy
so tell me how is it so bad
they would die for everything you have
be grateful
anytime you can.

When you look to the stars for help
when you feel so alone
just remember
you have a home
you have a bed
you have a place to rest your head
you have a job

you have a car
so wherever you are
be grateful
through all the scars.

So tell me
how is it so bad
they would die for everything you have
be grateful
anytime you can.

Jeff Oliver

{*Once Upon a Far Away Land*}

Once upon a place in a far away land,
a castle stood tall on a mountain of sand
an ocean front view where fish swim through,
a river of gold, or so I'm told

Where birds fly free in the sky so blue,
and a light from Heaven shines brightly through

The animals come to visit this place
and kiss the children on their face
a beautiful sight for everyone to see,
a magical place for the honeybee
where bedtime stories are read each night,
as the stars from Heaven light up the night

The dreams that take you to this place,
protect the children and put a smile on their face

When the morning comes to take you there,
the birds sing to the children that stop and stare

A fairy godmother takes you by the hand,
Once Upon a Far Away Land...

Donnie Pike

Heavens Answers

Something troubling has brought you here.
Your furrowed brow makes that clear.
Bow your head, and air your woes.
Up to Heaven let them go.

Guaranteed an answer you will receive.
Though it may be different than for which you plead.
There's a bigger plan than can be seen.
Yet on His love don't fail to lean.

Please take this message as a token of love.
And believe that He is listening from the Heavens above.

LK Pilgrim

Bravery

Grown men speak of their bravery,
What it means in their beliefs.
Tales of bruises and swinging fists,
Exultant in these various conquests.
Making themselves out to be kings
Because of some small victories.

A few bruises do not make a man.
Bravery is found with results of a bad scan.
It is found in the hearts in these beds.
In the dreams inside their heads.
The way their eyes are full of wonder.
In the encouragement given to each other.

What strength is found inside these walls
Will probably never be heard in concert halls.
Yet it consists of more maturity and grace
Than any song about patron saints.
You have the hopes of a million unknown friends
Wishing you victory in every prayer sent.

Stephen Remillard

"Revel in Survival"

She may be shattered, but never destroyed.
The steel in her spine has been forged in the flames
and she has emerged from the ashes,
triumphant in her rise and revival.

Her comeback is a testament to her warrior spirit;
refusing to submit to defeat by adversity.
She has returned resplendent in her strength,
and will forever revel in her survival.

Gypsy's_Reverie

A Sonnet

Whene're the worries of the day your attitude depress,
When bad news or harsh words you hear discourage and oppress;
When words meant to inspire you seem trite and so cliché:
"Chin up," "Take heart," "Be strong, my friend – today's a
brand-new day"

When problems all surround you, but solutions are unclear,
When life still throws at you its worst but yet there's more to fear;
When unanticipated loss bereaves us of what's dear,
When day begins with no real sense of hope, or joy, or cheer;

Stress threatens to engulf us, and dark mountains loom so steep,
but people tell you "just buck up" and "turn the other cheek -"
and you won't let them see you cry for fear they'll think you're weak.

Remember this, and breathe, my child, for you are not alone:
your worth is not something that you should ever have to prove.
All you need to know is that you're human, and are loved.

Vaughn Roste

'Fuck Cancer'

It's time to put to sleep
any bad blood
is no longer mine to keep
I'll turn the poison into stardust
focusing on my dreams
I'm growing Warrior Wings
while kicking this disease
I will put up a fight
keep my heart filled up with wishes
so if someday you see
my heartbeat's run out of kisses
Know I tried with all I am
to reclaim what Cancer stole
and you will always find my spirit
sleeping safe inside your soul

Michelle Schaper

Moments Lost

I get lost in little moments like these.
Dew drops hanging on bare branches,
And the falling of the leaves.

The soft sound of wind,
And squirrels playing in the trees.

Yes,
I get lost in little moments like these.

All by myself with no one around,
And although I get lost,
These are the moments I don't wish to be found

Dennis Shepherd

Hope

You are the brightest star in the universe.
The sunniest day without a cloud in the sky.
Determination is your saving grace.
There are angels lighting your way.
Illuminating the darkest of days.
Close your eyes...Remember how far you've come.
Rise up like the warrior that you are.

Pam Surface

Life Is Why We Rise

In Cancer, life becomes both the battle and the risk.
It's pain and suffering.
Finding strength in the bravest fight you'll ever fight.
A struggle in the heaviness of truth.
Life is more than just holding on to.
Sometimes it means letting go of a part of us.
Life, the purpose that gives us the will to fight.
But this fight is different.
There's a greatness to the battle fought, many simply can't understand.
It's something personal, when cancer attacks.
It isn't just a beast to slay.
It's a battle of body vs. mind.
Where a part of yourself has become the enemy.
To kill this insidious beast, one must sacrifice the very vessel, or its parts, in effort to stay alive.
For life, we do this.
Life becomes courage.
Life becomes hope.
Life becomes faith.
Donning a smile, the bravest act some days.
Cancer, an unforgiving beast that turns a part of us into our own enemy.
A war within ourselves.
Through parched lips, the chemical robs the very vessel that keeps the soul alive.
The soul fights to conquer through.
Days spent learning to let go, in effort to make it through.
Reverberation of aspiration shatters through the fear.
Fighting for life and the goodness it yields.
It's seeing life as the vision and bravely taking up the shield.

It's the embodiment of strength that resides in the eyes of a survivor.
In the face of all that is fought, the spark of determination becomes evermore alive.
The everglow of life, staking its claim
on moments you seek embark.
Victory against the beast that comes to leave it's awful mark.
Pick up the shield.
Look fear in the eyes.
No matter the sacrifice, life is why we rise.

Melissa A. Tafoya

Meteor Shower

A wish flashes across the sky,
trailed by blinding glory.
Eyes closed, breaths held,
it vanishes in a blink.

Hearts race across the moon
in buoyant anticipation.
Hope beyond hope
a granting of desire.

A flicker of childhood
held in ancient folklore,
unlocking forgotten joy.
A single blaze of light.

Believing, not believing,
we never abandon
the wonder in a moment,
wishing on a star.

Ann Christine Tabaka

Star Wishes

Where do our wishes go when we wish upon a star?
Do our words drift through empty space or tumble into a wishing jar
Do the heavens hear our wish and grant our meager pleas
Or do they go unheard and dance endlessly on a heavenly breeze
I choose to send my wishes there among the stars
Granted or not these wishes I wish are my heart's fondest memoirs

Diana L Thomas

"Dear Child"

tribulations unceasingly
rain down on you in
a loveless effort to attack
and break your aching body

yet grains of sand and truth
begin to take root in the depths
of your gentle soul
becoming tiny pearls

glorious in their minuscule splendor

Melody Wang

THE TICKING TIME BOMB:

It's what he said when he looked at me. Square in my eyes shot like a Canon.
This is lynch syndrome it's what I have.

Cancer causing genetic trait, well isn't that just great.
Well I thought I'm taking a stand. No genetic trait will determine my fate.

So I stand up straight and tall though my back is against a wall.
The opponent fierce with blood shot eyes. His look of death bores like ice.

A deep breath taken; slowly released. The opponent snarls with a growl.
Stained yellow teeth crookedly evil mocking my stand thinks I'm beat.
Little does he know who fights my war. My champion strikes and his aim is true.
The opponent falls and slinks away to pick his wounds for another day.

My champions name is quite famous. The one, the only, Lord Jesus.
Though current cancer is gone for now and two bouts I have both fought and won.
The evil opponent lurks in the shadows waiting for that bell to ring to show his ugly face once more.

Lord Jesus will be ready, with his sword polished and sharp.
To once again defend my body from the ravaging affect of a messed up gene.

Romans 8:37. Nay, in all these things we are more than conquers through him that loved us. 2 Tim 2:3 thou therefore endure hardness as a good soldier of Jesus Christ.

Christine S Weir

Little one

My dear little one
Wipe those tears from your eyes
Chase those monsters away
Don't let fear shut your heart
You shall be okay, dear one

Run free, there are no gates
Let your laughter bring joy
Find content in your dreams
Make books good friends
Stay humble little one

The world can swallow you whole
Know who you are
You have come so far
Don't just follow blindly
You are uniquely you

Keep your eye on hope
Your spirit free
Joy your driving force
Self-love your strength
Most of all, know your worth

Let them frown

Let them wonder

Never let them change who you are!

By Hanlie Wheeler

Will Be

It won't be much longer until we can take you home,
To be with your family so you can grow strong.
You can play with the puppies, the kittens too,
And run through the yard like you used to do.
It will happen again just you wait and see,
You will be home with us,
With your Family.

Linda J Zimmerman

www.ingramcontent.com/pod-product-compliance
Ingram Content Group UK Ltd.
Pitfield, Milton Keynes, MK11 3LW, UK
UKHW020137250726
13967UKWH00002B/715